Never
in a
loving
way

Josie Byrnes

First published in 1977 by The Gatehouse Project
Reprinted 1978, 1979, 1982, 1987
and in 1994 by Gatehouse Books Ltd

Editor, Stella Fitzpatrick
Cover design, David Andrassy
Photograph page 16, Roger Mayne
Illustrations page 10, Angela Brown; pages12 & 18, Josie Byrnes

Published and distributed by Gatehouse Books Ltd,
Hulme Adult Education Centre, Hulme Walk, Manchester M15 5FQ

Printed by L Lawlor, Huddersfield Road/Cross Street. Oldham OL4 1JX

ISBN 0 906253 01 2
British Library cataloguing in publication data:
A catalogue record for this book is available from the British Library

Gatehouse is grateful
for continued financial support
from Manchester City Council
and North West Arts Board

north west arts board

Manchester
making it happen
CENTRAL GRANTS TEAM
SUPPORTED BY
Manchester
CITY COUNCIL

Gatehouse is a member of the Federation of Worker Writers & Community Publishers

We have planned the book
so that left hand-pages
tell my full story.
Right-hand pages
tell my story too,
but in a shorter way,
so you can take a break
at a point that makes sense.

Josie Byrnes

Poor and hungry

I can remember when I was a little child. Well, I suppose most people can remember when they was a little child. But I came from a poor family and I know what it's like to be poor and hungry and to have no bed. Yes, I can see it now, as my mother used to lay us down on the floor, with coats for a mattress, and coats over us for blankets and sheets and even one for a pillow, a coat rolled up.

Quite often my father, he was out of work because he couldn't walk. It was some form of rheumatism he had. Even when my mother went to work we never got hardly anything to eat. I don't know why. I think she really got fed up because my father didn't show any interest in her, because he wouldn't allow her to have any electric and there was no hot water. The only thing we had was gas and candlelight, and that wasn't much use with five young children to watch. I don't know why.

He even told me I didn't have to learn to read and write because of the simple reason I was a girl and would grow up to be married and have babies.

1

I can remember
when I was a little child
I came from a poor family
and I know what it's like
to be poor and hungry
and to have no bed.
Yes, I can see it now,
as my mother used to lay us down
on the floor
with coats for a mattress
and coats over us
for blankets and sheets
and even one for a pillow,
a coat rolled up.

Well, I did grow up and I found life was horrible. I often sit back and wonder why I was never given a chance. But now I can tell you why. I was one of the many dirty children. I couldn't cope with life. I don't know how come I couldn't cope with it.

I also suffered with my eyes. There were times when my sisters could stand in front of me and I would not see them. There were times when the teacher put something on the blackboard, I never had it down. I had to laugh many a time about the trouble I got into, copying sums down. Don't ask me how I got the wrong thing down, but I did do.

Everything was dark

Well, to start back from being little, the first time in my life I can remember sitting in the classroom writing, (well, not writing, the teacher asking us if we knew how to write) I can remember sitting down scribbling on a piece of paper, till she says she would have to learn me. The next time I can remember sitting with a shade over my left eye because I could not see with my right eye. She used to bring the roof down on me because I used to lift the shade up for fear of the dark.

I wondered why
I was never given a chance.
But now I can tell you why.
I was one of the many dirty children.
I couldn't cope with life.
I also suffered with my eyes.
There were times
when my sisters could stand
in front of me
and I would not see them.
There were times
when the teacher put something
on the blackboard,
I never had it down.

Then in front of me she would place a book and tell me there was a nice little book for me to read. I couldn't even see the classroom wall, because everything was dark, never mind read a book. Besides, I couldn't read.

Then for two years I was out of school. I can't remember them two years. It must have been two years because my parents tell me. It was because of my eyes I couldn't go to school. They said they couldn't accept the responsibility.

I can't tell you much about them two years, whether I slept on the damp floor or what, or maybe we had a bed then. I remember going back to school and I didn't have a bed.

"There's no nothing!"

Yes, that's when I can remember when the coats came into my life. I don't expect that teacher wanted to teach me. I was always a lousy headed little girl. I was always scruffy.

In front of me
the teacher would place a book
and tell me
there was a nice little book
for me to read.
I couldn't even see the classroom wall
because everything was dark.
Besides, I couldn't read.

Then my sister Molly was supposed to have looked after us. My God, she didn't. My mother went out to work. My father was working at the time. Molly would get us up and then go back to sleep. She never washed us or did nowt for us.

Then we'd come home at dinner-time. There were four of us, but two of them were never there. They must have stayed at school for dinners.

Sometimes there was an old chair there and there she would curl herself up and go to sleep. Other times she would curl up on the floor. We were greeted with, "There's no sugar, there's no butter, there's no bread, there's no milk."

Then she would lay down again. A few minutes afterwards my sister, looking proper gormless and putting on a sleepy voice, would add, "There's no nothing." So I went to school hungry again. No breakfast and quite often of a night-time there was nowt to eat.

Then we'd come home
at dinner time.
My sister Molly was supposed
to look after us.
My God, she didn't.
We were greeted with,
"There's no sugar,
there's no butter,
there's no bread,
there's no milk,
there's no nothing."
So I went to school hungry again.

Swinging happily in the park

Yes, I know what life is like, how cruel it can be. But it also has its funny side, like the time I played truant from school. Well, it's not really funny now, but it was. Within seconds of me not going to school, there was a man at the house,
"Where is she?"
My mother replied, "I've sent Josie to school."
"But she's not there."
I had dodged, and there she found me, swinging happily in the park. Oh, I had to walk past the school to get to the park, and I did do!

People make fun of you

But nobody knowed, not even the teachers know what it's like when you're a child and you can't speak properly, when people make fun of you and mock you, which happened to me. And there's no-one at home to help them. I suppose you'll be saying by now, "Well, what was the point in giving you an education if you wasn't going to be helped at home?"

One day, My mother found me
swinging happily in the park

I had dodged school.

The point is, if you don't help people like myself, it grow up with them. Most of them find it hard when they grow up, to cope with life.

The teacher always used to be saying I couldn't do this, and I coudn't do the other, and perhaps I still believe I can't. Half the time I've got to fight myself. Oh aye, yes, now I'm grown up and living with it.

A very big doll's house

I tell you something else they did to me. Every Christmas time, I got nothing for Christmas. So, the teacher decided after we went back, to ask us what we got for Christmas. I heard them all say about their doll's pram, the doll's house and what have you. Oh, I always had them. "Have you, Josie?" she used to reply.
"Oh, yes Miss, but my mother wouldn't let me take them out."

I can remember one particular week, I told her I had a very big doll's house, big enough to live in. And it had an electric light and furniture. I said it was nearly as big as our house.

Every Christmas time,
I got nothing for Christmas.
After we went back to school,
the teacher decided to ask us
what we got for Christmas.

J. Byrnes

I told her I had a very big doll's house,
big enough to live in.
And it had electric light
and furniture.

The teacher said, "Do you take it out to play with?"
I said, "No, Miss, my mother won't let me."

That week we had nowt to eat and if I can
remember correctly, we hadn't had anything to eat
the week before. What lies you can be made to tell
when teacher helps it along. I don't think children
should be praised and asked what they got for
Christmas, or asked to draw it, because some of
them unfortunate children have got nothing. How can
you tell people that no-one is looking after you and
you want help? As a child you don't really think
about help.

Tide marks on my neck

Oh yes, I've had all that, even standing in the snow
with a thin summer frock on. It's hard to believe,
when it was winter and the wind was blowing. I've
got to admit, they were kind enough with me, the
teachers then. They used to let me in near the warm
pipe. Ten or even twenty minutes is a long time to
wait in the cold without warm clothes.

As a child
you don't really think about help.
How can you tell everybody
that you slept on the floor,
your bed was the floor with coats?
How can you tell people
that no-one is looking after you
and you want help?

It's also wrong to hold it over a child, to treat them differently because they are poor, like they treated me. I remember the time I went with tide marks on my neck, and the teacher played holy hell with me, shaking me, shouting at me, making fun of me. Yet when my mother went up, she said she didn't blame my mother, she blamed me. And yet my mother hadn't ever bothered to see I'd had a wash. She hadn't even bothered to tell me that I was dirty. She'd just let me run out.

The horriblest headmaster

Then I went to secondary school. I've got to admit I did not like it. To me, he was the horriblest headmaster going. He had a couple of times hit me across the face because I was never clean. I washed my face and my arms, but never my legs. And I remember one particular day, I ran out, and one of the teachers got hold of me and brought me back. He wasn't a bad teacher, but I didn't like him. And my mother came up to see the headmaster. She said, "You do more than I dare do." But my mother did a lot. Admittedly, she didn't belt us one. But she would send me to the shop dirty.

16

I would say, "I want to have a wash."

"Oh no, you're lovely and clean Josie, lovely and clean."

Someone would say something about me being dirty, and it would get back to her. She'd say that I was yapping, that I tell the neighbours everything. I didn't have a chance to tell the neighbours anything. I was too afeared of it getting back to her, too feared of her nagging and carrying on at me.

Besides, I knew what the neighbours was like. They'd give you a butty and they'd say you was starving. Admittedly, I was starving, as a child. So was many other people.

My first Christmas tree

I'm going to tell you something now, and I quite often sit back and think about it. I can remember the very first Christmas tree we got. It was the very first thing my mother kept her promise about. I had a friend I ran around with, this girl Carol Jones, and her mother was the very worst one. If she gave you a butty, a jam butty, which I don't think anything of, she'd say you were starving.

17

I can remember the very first
 Christmas tree we got.
It was the very first thing
 my mother kept her promise about.

I mean if I give a jam butty to a child, I don't say that they're always starving.

Anyway, my mother said to me, "Why do you hang around with Carol Jones?"

So I said, "Well, I want someone to play with."

She said, "I know why. Every Christmas time, you hang around her. Every Christmas. It's to look at that Christmas tree they've got."

I don't know why, but she said, "I'll get you a Christmas tree, but I cannot get anything else to go with it. There will be no silver balls, no lights, no candles. If I get you the Christmas tree, will you promise to keep away from her?"

I kept away from her for a few weeks. That weekend I got my Christmas tree!

And that was my first Christmas tree. I was fourteen when I got it, and it was the best Christmas I ever had. Oh, I know what you're thinking, I'm barmy. Well, maybe I am. But believe me, I'm not. It's the people in the world that's stuck their noses up at me, sneered at me when I was poor and only a child, that turned me like this.

My mother said,
"I'll get you a Christmas tree,
but I cannot get anything else
to go with it.
There will be no silver balls,
no lights,
no candles."

Living in a dream world

I tell you something else. We used to pretend, my sister and I, that my mother and father wasn't our mother and father! They was our auntie and uncle! Oh, we came from America! Oh, what our father and mother would do if they knew, only knew how our uncle and auntie were treating us! They would go mad! Another favourite was that I had a wardrobe and I had lost the key and we couldn't get our new clothes out of it. We never had any new clothes!

Well, I took to living in a dream world where I could become the top, and people were friendly with me. Oh yes, I were clever, so clever even the teacher was asking me the questions. I don't know how, but I was top of the class! I was always so clever.Yes, we had this and we had the other.

That was my green world and I learnt to live with it. Even now, my husband has got to wake me up. And he always says, "Come on now, don't say it. Back to your green world again. Dreaming, sleeping, all day."

I took to living in a dream world
where I could become top,
and people were friendly with me.
Oh, yes, I were clever,
so clever even the teacher
was asking me the questions.

But there was a whole happy place I lived in. And it was the only place I could become top and equal. Don't ask me why, but do you know what it's like? Do you know what it's like to be unsure of yourself? Well, I do.

Fear stopped me

I try not to day-dream. But I still say it's the most friendly place in the world. It was the only place I could turn to as a child.

But I can remember the last year I was at school. I did really want to learn to read and write and be like the other children and I wanted to cry out and ask for help, but I thought, "If they go to my mother," which they would have done, in them days, "going back and seeing her, she'll have my life, she'll play holy hell with me. They'll say I've been yapping. They'll say I've done this and I've done the other." Fear stopped me. So when I left school, I was able to read only a little bit and unable to speak properly, until I got married.

I try not to day-dream
but I still say
it's the most friendly place
in the world.
It was the only place
I could turn to
as a child.

"Father, mother and husband to you"

And I remember my husband telling me three years after we'd been married, he said, "I've had to be father, mother and husband to you. I had to discipline you and I had to give you mother love where your mother hadn't given it to you." Oh yes, everyone knowed it. They all used to say my mother didn't really love me.

Never in a loving way

Maybe she had cause to. I can remember her talking when I really got a bit older, about her and my father having a big row. I've never told people before. Anyway, my father walked out. Well, my father told the same story. But he told me he had nowhere to go, and no sooner had he lain down and gone off to sleep, and I would appear before him. He said, "Josie, go home. Go home, Josie, I can't find a place for myself. You go home, love, to your mammy. That's a good little girl." He gets up and moves away. Oh, he came home alright, to tell my mother he hadn't come back for her sake, only for mine. I don't know whether my mother hated me after that, but I certainly don't

I can remember
my mother talking
about her and my father
having a big row.
My father walked out.
But he told me
he had nowhere to go,
and no sooner had he
gone off to sleep,
and I would appear before him.

remember her loving me. I certainly can never remember her cuddling me, only the time she used to stroke my hair when other people were there and say I was her baby, to look as if she loved me. Stroked my hair, my head, but never in a loving way. She must have thought I was the most horrible child going. You may ask how old was I when he walked out? No more than twelve months old!

They was horrible and cruel to me in more than one way. They didn't bring me up like I should have been. They didn't help me grow up. Yet I loved them. I can't see any fault in them now, including my mother. But as a child, I used to ask my father, "Was she my mother?" I felt so ill-treated by her.

There was times in the middle of the night when she got me up to find the time. She would never believe me. I could never convince her that everyone was in bed. There were times when she sent me to the shop where she owed money, to get stuff on tick. The answer would be, "No," which is quite natural. You don't expect to owe people money and get tick.

I remember my husband telling me,
"I had to give you mother love
where your mother
hadn't given it to you."
I don't remember
my mother loving me,
never remember her cuddling me,
the only time she used to
stroke my hair
was when other people were there
and say I was her baby
to look as if she loved me.

Well, she would never believe me. She would say, "You're a liar. Go back, go back." I went back.

Mind you, I don't blame my mother because when she went down herself, the fellow would hand her the stuff over. So it did make out I was a liar. Well, it did look like that, didn't it? Even though I'd been in there. But you see, I didn't have the sense to say, "You refused me!" I didn't like to be cheeky. But I've learnt the hard way.

You're not so perfect yourself

But I still go back to my green world. Even now. And I'm afraid if being educated means turning out like a lot of people is turning out, I don't want it. I don't want it at all, because it's an evil way. People are unfriendly and don't want to be friendly. Well, you're going to ask, "Why, what's that got to do with it? People have got to defend themselves." Yes, you can defend yourself and still be friendly.

You can always help someone who's slow. I don't mean do the work for them. But always remember, never make fun of people. If you think back, you're

I still go back to my green world,
even now.
And I'm afraid that
if being educated
means turning out
like a lot of people is turning out,
I don't want it at all,
because it's an evil way.
You can always help someone
who's slow.

not so perfect yourself, are you? If you look at your self, you're not so perfect.

I've learnt a lot in forty years. Most of it since I've been married. Well, how did I help my children? Well, I haven't. I failed them as a mother for the simple reason that because I did not know this and I don't know the other, I haven't been able to speak or to read properly. Oh, I'm learning and I'm going to learn. But I hope that by learning I'm not going to be hateful to some of them who haven't got an education. I hope I can still see folk for what they are and not make fun of people.

I've learnt a lot in forty years,
but I hope that by learning
I'm not going to be hateful
to some of them
who haven't got an education.
I hope I can still see folk
for what they are
and not make fun of people.

Gatehouse Books

Gatehouse is a unique publisher

Our writers are adults who are developing their basic reading and writing skills. Their ideas and experiences make fascinating material for any reader, but are particularly relevant for adults working on their reading and writing skills. The writing strikes a chord - a shared experience of struggling against many odds.

The format of our books is clear and uncluttered. The language is familiar and the text is often line-broken, so that each line ends at a natural pause.

Gatehouse books are both popular and respected within adult basic education throughout the English speaking world. They are also a valuable resource within secondary schools, special needs education, social services and within the prison education service and probation service.

Booklist available

Gatehouse Books
Hulme Adult Education Centre
Hulme Walk
Manchester M15 5FQ
Tel: 061 226 7152

A donation of £1.00 towards the cost of the booklist and postage, would be appreciated.

The Gatehouse Publishing Charity is a registered charity reg no 1011042. Gatehouse Books Ltd is a company limited by guarantee reg no. 2619614